Crystal & Gem Magick

BOOKS BY AISLIN

TAROT DECIPHERED
ASHLING WICCA, BOOK ONE
ASHLING WICCA, BOOK ONE: THE WORKBOOK
ASHLING WICCA, BOOK TWO
ASHLING WICCA, BOOK TWO: THE WORKBOOK
ASHLING WICCA, BOOK THREE
ASHLING WICCA, BOOK THREE: THE WORKBOOK

*FORTHCOMING

Crystal & Gem Magick

Aislin

For Heather
Thanks for listening.
I know I was driving you nutty.
It is a testament to your grace that
you never said anything about it.

Table of Contents

Introduction

Crystals and gemstones have always been with us in some form or another. Ever since we stepped from the cave we sought to use nature's abundant minerals to our advantage. Though it would be some time before we would discover the glittering bounty inside the earth, one of our first tools was stone. Before we slipped a stray bit of quartz into a leather pouch, we were using natural stone and rock for many things. From a purely mundane standpoint, stone could be fashioned into tools for cutting, hunting, grinding, and hammering. It became a weapon of defense and protection. Eventually it was even used to make war on our enemies. Much later, and after some experimentation, different minerals were crushed into powder and used as dyes or cosmetics.

Beyond the strictly functional, the many stones and gems found in nature took on another roll. They became intrinsically linked to religion, spirituality, and magick. Stones were found in unusual shapes or varieties and worn or carried for various purposes. Soon shapes and images were carved or fashioned intentionally from raw stone sources. Idols, statues, amulets, and eventually temples were created in stone and decorated with gemstones and crystals. As humanity spread and grew, learning how to explore and better understand our surrounding environment, we began to discover, catalogue, and assign various powers and meanings to the multitude of different crystals and gemstones we encountered.

At the same time, a new factor was introduced into our understanding of the stone kingdom…rarity. Hand in hand with rarity came value, and the nature of our interaction with stones became intertwined with status, finance, and even politics. But despite the stone's entrance into the world of social hierarchy, it retained its ability to enchant. By the time civilization had progressed beyond the age of superstition, the gemstone was too entangled in legend to be entirely stripped of its magickal properties. To this day, no book on the subject, however scientific in tries to be, is without at least a passing tribute to the mystical nature of gemstones. Most include a nod to the legendary healing properties of gems, and nearly all refer at least in passing to the zodiacal correspondences of the birthstone. This is gem magick, and it is a part of our world whether we want to believe it or not. It is one of the few forms of magick that is not dependent upon our belief.

In the modern age, where humanity is once again taking a serious look at its mystical past, the power of crystals and gems has been granted another serious inspection. There is no denying the tendency of humans to become fascinated by the gems that surround them. Together we share a long history of partnership and symbolism. But what is it about the nature of these glittering beauties that encourages us to use them as spiritual or magickal tools? Perhaps some of that answer lies in the stones themselves. They're just so pretty. But surely that isn't all there is to it.

Surprisingly to some, modern science itself can help us to a fuller understanding of how and why gem magick works, and why we're so fascinated with it. When all the technical sources on gemology shamelessly refer to the gemstone's magickal past, how is it that so few of the magickal texts on stones touch even remotely on gem science? It has always been the way of the gemstone to occupy both a mundane and a spiritual role, and to do so with flourish even as it claims both worlds as its own. It seems quite appropriate, then, to approach the subject of gem magick with an attitude that is open to both the traditional spiritual aspects of the stones and the practical nature of gem science.

If the physical elements are the building blocks of our universe, minerals are their first creation. The stones, gems, and crystals we encounter today have literally been forming for thousands of years deep within the earth. But what differentiates a gem from a rock? There is a hierarchy of elemental purity that comes into play here. Physical elements, such as carbon and hydrogen, combine to form minerals. Minerals then combine to form rock. Most of the items we term 'gems' fall into the mineral category, indicating that their composition is made up of relative few elements. Minerals are also characterized by a geometric and regular arrangement at the atomic level. This is specifically true of the crystal form of any mineral, which displays outwardly the geometric pattern of the atomic structure.

How does this translate into the world of gem and crystal magick? First, during the process of mineral formation, the material is subjected to intense energy levels. The chemical and physical properties of gems have been proven to facilitate the storage and emission of energy, heat, and light. Though this effect is most studied in reference to quartz and quartz crystals for both industrial and magickal use, it has been documented in many other gem types. Secondly, the process of creating gems (naturally or artificially) relies on the cooperation of the four magickal elements. Water carries the dissolved elements to the formation site. Fire is the heat needed to change and fuse the elements together. Earth is the pressure and the presence of raw elements, without which the gemstone could not be fashioned. And air is the space within the host rock for the minerals to collect and form.

From a magickal standpoint, then, it is not difficult to see the sudden significance of a tool that represents a balance of the four natural elements, resonates and stores energy by its very nature, and incorporates a rare purity and geometry in its physical structure. Add to this inherent tendency the rich history and legends surrounding the spiritual world of gems and you get one of the most powerful and enduring magickal traditions of all time.

Stone Selection

From the first time someone picks up a shiny stone, rubs the dust and sediment from it, and discovers they hold a gem or crystal, there is an emotional relationship. Despite all reason, and without any true scientific basis, every major culture in history has paid tribute to gemstones in one form or another. People throughout the ages have sold all they own, and indeed sold themselves, for a single stone. The ownership and display of certain gems has been limited to the nobility and often indicated social status, wealth, and political alignment. Men have faced exile, hardship, war, and even death for the chance to possess their stone of choice. Considering the legendary powers of gems, it is no wonder we have a special place in our hearts for the illusive and variable world of precious stones. They have been said to heal, protect, grant invisibility, and even provide true immortality. Unfortunately, hand in hand with the history, glamour, and legends of these stones is a modern industry that is also rich in deceit, deception, theft, and fraud.

Discussions on crystal and gem magick often ignore, overlook, or dismiss this aspect of the topic. As an individual pursuing a working relationship with gems as a magickal tool, however, it is vital to acquire at least a passing understanding of the mundane side of purchasing and selling stones. While it may be noble to assume that the lovely amethyst purchased at the new age store down the road is exactly as it was represented, most magickal people would be seriously shocked to know that the deep purple color of their tumbled gem is most likely not natural, but the result of dyeing. The fabulous black onyx ring they had such a deal on at the shop on the corner? Well…nearly *all* black onyx is actually dyed chalcedony and not onyx at all. If you got a great deal on onyx, it's probably not onyx.

Before you become depressed and demoralized, understand one thing. The dyed amethyst, or onyx that is really chalcedony, or that smoky topaz that is actually a cloudy quartz, are all perfectly acceptable stones to use in gem magick. What is most important getting what you're paying for. If a stone's true nature, treatments, fabrications, and even dye jobs are revealed at the time of purchase, and the price reflects all these things, then the person acquiring the stone is fully aware of what they are purchasing, can make an informed decision, and is getting a fair deal. The danger lies in being sold a stone presented as natural that is, in fact, not what you expect. This becomes glaringly true when you purchase an expensive stone only to find the exact stone, or a superior one, at the mundane lapidary or rock store down the street for half the price.

While a detailed inspection of stone treatments (legitimate and shady) is not really the point of this book, there are some simple steps to take to avoid beginning your relationship with a magickal gem on a negative note. Primarily, I recommend reading a good book on gem treatments and synthetics. If you have a specific stone (amethyst, for example) that you work with or purchase frequently, it would also be a good idea to keep up on any news concerning that particular stone. For example, as amethyst mining is producing less and less stones of good dark color, the intensely purple stone on sale for a single dollar is most likely going to be dyed. A natural deep amethyst is actually very expensive and will not be sold for a dollar. Become an informed consumer and it becomes more difficult for you to be fooled.

Secondly, and once armed with a good base knowledge about gems, ask questions. If the sign says "amethyst" ask outright if it's natural and where it came from. Is the color natural? Has the stone been enhanced or treated? Odds are if you have a reputable business, your questions will receive prompt, friendly answers.

Chances are also good that the answer will be, "I have no idea." This is especially true in stores that are not specifically rock or jewelry stores. It is also likely that persons in non-jewelry stores will have no idea and will still tell you the stone is natural rather than admit they don't know. That being said, I don't want to give a negative impression of any stores or discourage you from shopping at these perfectly fine businesses. Most often the intention is not to deceive and the false information is given in ignorance. Be informed yourself because it's the best chance you'll have of spotting the stone you're after. You might even be able to avoid being ripped off.

Before we move on to the more uplifting aspects of stone selection, I must address one more aspect of the stone trade: acceptable enhancement. While no stone should be sold without disclosure of any treatments or enhancements, there are some techniques that are so prevalent and accepted in the gem world that they are rarely even mentioned during a transaction. Heat-treating is a prime example of this and the wide majority of stones (over 90%) of certain types (ruby and sapphire come immediately to mind) are heat treated to intensify color. Purchasing a heated stone without knowing it is far from a tragedy. The enhancements to watch for are ones that may be less than permanent. Oiling, dying, radiating, layering, backing, and painting are the big worries. The problem with these being that months or years down the road the stone's appearance could change drastically, usually for the worse.

Despite the above warnings, obtaining stones for magickal work can be a fun and joyous undertaking. Whether you receive your stones as gifts, purchase them wisely, find them by accident along a path, or delve into the fabulous world of rock-hunting and amateur mining, the rewards are immeasurable. Today new types of stones and new colors and varieties of those gems we've used for years are abundant and constantly being discovered. Advances in gem science and art have led to an extensive array of new 'fancy cuts' and fantasy shapes that are awe-inspiring and stunningly beautiful. All of these new discoveries have exciting implications for the future of gem magick and spiritual learning.

With such a wide array to choose from, the task of selecting stones for magickal work can seem a bit overwhelming. The person who loves a deep red garnet, for instance, may be slightly taken aback when they discover that the gem is now available in green, pink, and orange as well as the more traditional red. How do new colors of a well-known gem fit into the traditional spiritual meanings of the stone? How does a natural rough stone compare magickally to one that has been carefully faceted and polished? How important are the inclusions and imperfections common in a stone like emerald? These are only a few of the questions that become obvious after a tentative step into the gem universe.

Intrigued by the above myself, I decided to design a little test. I set out a series of gems on a table and asked blindfolded volunteers to choose between groups of pre-selected stones based on their energy 'feel.' Though the results of these experiments are hardly scientific evidence toward any conclusion, I found it interesting that while some tests supported the traditional ideals of gem magick, others diverged enough to warrant closer inspection.

Most surprising, in my opinion, were the tests concerning the effects of color versus the chemical composition. Traditionally stones are associated with magickal properties based in a large part upon their color correspondences. So green stones are often associated with healing and growth, pink with love, black with protection, and on and on. This would suggest a green garnet would fall nicely into a 'healing' category, while its deep red counterpart would remain primarily associated with energy, passion and vigor.

The gem test in which I asked subjects to handle various colored stones of the same type indicated no discernable pattern in stone selection. But the test in which the same individuals held several similarly colored stones where only one was of a different type entirely, and thus of an entirely different chemical make-up, was astounding. Three out of four people picked the single different stone out of four. This is exactly the opposite of what I had expected because I had assumed that color played the most significant role in stone properties.

It must be noted, however that the subjects of the tests were blindfolded. In practical use, the visual effects of color cannot be denied and I suspect that a combination of color and type will give us the most accurate interpretation of a stone's properties. So could a green garnet have a healing effect on issues associated with passion and vigor? It's entirely possible. By combining traditional meanings of color and type, can new, more fine-tuned, uses be discovered? It seems likely that as we uncover new types and varieties our ability to incorporate them into magickal systems will grow rapidly.

In the cases in which subjects were asked to pick between faceted and natural stones the results seem to be mixed. Though most individuals chose the natural geometric crystal over a faceted gem, the gem won out resoundingly over a rounded rough stone. All stones presented were of same variety and color. From comments left by test subjects, the geometric angles of both the natural crystal form and the human faceted gem helped to intensify and direct energy. The rough stone, though still usable, did not direct energy with quite the same intensity.

This is not surprising considering facets of a cut stone are calculated to direct and reflect light entering and exiting the gem. The action of this reflected light is what causes a stone to have brilliance and sparkle. If we agree that energy responds to physical stimuli, it seems possible that it too can be reflected and directed within a gem via the faceting.

Faceted gems are immensely useful in crystal and gem magick. To understand why, think about how a rough stone becomes a faceted gem. A rough stone is honed and cut in a precise way to deepen, intensify, and best display the color and beauty of the stone. This is also true of the cabochon, or non-faceted, cut. This suggests that while rough or tumbled stones are perfectly functional for magickal purposes, there is no need to shy away from cut or polished gems. In fact, there may be a lot of benefit to be had from incorporating faceted stones into magickal work. They have great power and can direct energy with more efficiency than their rough counterparts. The downside is faceted gems are quite expensive. But if you can find them at a reasonable cost, it would make sense to take advantage of their brilliance and use them in your magickal work.

The one thing that was glaringly obvious within both my tests and the accompanying research I couldn't quit reading is that the final choice of a stone for magickal use is a highly individual decision. As with any tool, it is also a very intuitive process and there isn't necessarily a right or wrong choice. No matter how suitable a perfectly cut stone could be for magickal working, if *you* don't feel right about using it, you shouldn't. If the natural stone is your choice, then it is the correct choice for you. This brings us back to our dyed piece of amethyst mentioned near the beginning of this section. Regardless of the quality or authenticity of a stone, if *you* have a strong emotional attachment to it, then it is the right stone for you.

One last word on selecting your stones. Get to know stones as much as possible. Arrange to visit jewelry stores, stone shops, rock museums, and even mines if at all possible. Expose yourself to a wide variety and you will begin to see the range of what is available to you even within a single type of stone. As you develop an eye for crystals and gems, be certain to handle as many specimens as you can manage. Learn to detect the subtle vibrations of a stone's stored energy. Practice with common rocks from your yard. The more of a 'feel' you have for stone energy, the more likely you will be to recognize the tell-tale 'zing' when you pick up the gem that is destined to be your personal magickal tool. Practice makes perfect, as the saying goes, so don't give up if you don't feel anything at first.

Stone Varieties

Most stones the magickal practitioner is likely to become involved with fall into one of three categories: precious gems, semi-precious gems, and ornamental stones. These categories cover nearly all minerals that at one time or another have been used by man for adornment purposes. A few minerals that are industrial or not commonly used by man may be of interest to the magickally inclined, but they are not seen often enough to be covered here. While this short book does not have the scope to cover an inclusive alphabetical listing of all magickal stones and properties, we will cover some popular and commonly found stones in the magickal world.

There are only four gemstone species that can be officially classified as "precious" according to the jewelry industry. Throughout history some semi-precious stones have made brief appearances on this list and then fallen out of popularity or were suddenly in enough supply to warrant removal. In most cases, the list of precious gems will be limited to the four that never seem to get off the list. Diamonds, emeralds, rubies and sapphires. These four will be more expensive than all others, so if you can't afford one of these, there are others you can use instead.

To make navigating this list a little easier, I've alphabetized this list (except for quartz; it's out of place, but quartz is special). You should feel free to research the stones you pick more thoroughly and perhaps mix and match to your heart's content.

- Agate – strength, bravery
- Alexandrite – luck, love
- Amber – luck, healing, protection
- Amethyst – dreams, psychic powers

- Aquamarine – psychic powers, purification
- Aventurine – mental powers, money
- Bloodstone – healing, strength
- Calcite – spirituality
- Carnelian – protection, peace
- Cat's Eye – wealth, beauty
- Citrine – protection
- Diamond – spirituality
- Emerald – money, love
- Fluorite – mental powers
- Garnet – healing, strength
- Hematite – healing, divination
- Jade – love, healing
- Jasper – health, beauty
- Lapis lazuli – joy, love
- Moonstone – divination, psychic powers
- Opal – astral projection
- Ruby – wealth, power
- Sapphire – love, meditation
- Topaz – protection, healing
- Quartz – protection, healing, power

There is one stone on the list above that is not like all the others. Quartz, just plain quartz, is an excellent all-purpose magickal stone. Colorless and easily programmed to any intent or need, a simple quartz can take the place of most other stones quite nicely. Even with a nice set of gems, even one of every other stone on the above list, I recommend keeping some quartz points on hand. There is also no substitute for a nice big clear quartz point as an energy directing tool.

In addition to the inherent qualities and powers mentioned above, there are two basic energies that stones possess. They are either projective, or receptive. Projective stones tend to be strong, bright, and forceful. Receptive stones are calm, inward, and peaceful.

Projective stones are masculine in nature and can be used in healing, protection, intellectual powers, luck, success, will power, courage, and for self-confidence.

Some projective stones are black, brown and red agate, amber, apache tears, aventurine, bloodstone, carnelian, cat's-eye, citrine, cross stone, diamond, garnet, red jasper, lava, obsidian, onyx, opal, ruby, sardonyx, sunstone, tiger's-eye, red tourmaline, and zircon.

Receptive stones are feminine in nature and can be used for soothing, love, wisdom, compassion, eloquence, sleep, dreams, friendship, growth, fertility, prosperity, spirituality, psychic ability, mysticism.

Some receptive stones are blue lace and green agate, amethyst, aquamarine, azurite, blue calcite, pink calcite, chrysocolla, chrysoprase, coal, coral, cross stone, quartz crystal, emerald, fossils, jade, brown and green jasper, jet, lapis lazuli, malachite, moonstone, mother-of-pearl, olivine, opal, pearl, peridot, salt, sapphire, blue, green and pink tourmaline, and turquoise.

But owning some pretty stones just isn't enough. You have to know how to take care of them. And that brings us to the next section.

Care & Maintenance

There are certain steps that assist in preparing stones for magickal work, including cleansing, charging, programming, and simply building a relationship with the stone as a tool. Equally as important, however, are some mundane precautions that should be carefully observed with your newly acquired gems.

Gems are partially rated according to durability. In fact, all minerals are sorted by hardness according to the Moh's Hardness Scale. Each stone is assigned a number from one to ten indicating how hard the material is in relation to any other. The practical importance of this list is simple. Any stone will scratch stones below it on the list and be scratched by any stone above it on the list. So this means that tucking a nice piece of quartz (Moh's 7) into a pouch with your favorite fluorite (Moh's 4) will result in a nice quartz and a pile of powdered Fluorite at worst. At the very least the Fluorite could be damaged in appearance. So if you are building spell bags or amulets consisting of a number of small inexpensive stones that you have no intention of retrieving, mix away. However, if you are using nice or expensive stones, or those that you have a strong attachment too, pay attention to hardness. Store stones separately or with others of similar rating. Remember too that hardness does not always indicate toughness. The diamond is the hardest stone in existence (Moh's 10) but extremely brittle and subject to cracking. Avoid any knocks, bumps, or rough treatment of your stones. Even a tough stone that is hit along a cleavage plane will break quite easily.

Some stones are affected by light or temperature and others, such as pearl, can be adversely affected by chemicals such as cosmetics and even hand lotion. It's always a good idea to store stones away from bright light and to avoid exposure to extreme temperatures. Finally, avoid using chemical or ultra-sonic cleaners unless you are absolutely positive the stone's color is natural and won't be affected. Oiled emeralds, as well as filled or otherwise treated stones can come out looking worlds worse than they went in. It's also important that you not handle your stones if your hands are still sticky from hand lotion. These chemicals can cause lasting damage to your stones.

Cleansing

By the time your new stone makes it into your hands, it has had quite a journey. Unless you found or mined the gem yourself, your knowledge of that journey is limited and based on speculation. Unfortunately, some of the tumbled and faceted stones that arrive on the retail market (and even the rough stones, for that matter) are harvested in a non-environmentally friendly manner. Stones pass through many hands along the way, and are exposed to many situations and different energies as well. Considering that our intentions are to utilize the energies stored in the stone, it becomes necessary to perform a cleansing on each new stone before it is used for magickal purposes.

There are a plethora of techniques to employ for cleansing stones and crystals. One of the simplest is to run the stone under a stream of running water, visualizing the negativity of any stored energy washing away. Alternately, stones can be soaked for three days in clear spring water, buried in the earth (or a pot of earth) for three days, set in salt (use caution, salt can be harsh) or flower petals for a time, or exposed to sunlight or moonlight for a set period. Usually three day, but sometimes up to the full cycle of the moon (a month).

One method that is consistent and can be used with any of the above is a simple visualization. Hold the stone to be cleansed in your palms and center yourself. Breathe deeply and try to connect with the 'feel' of the stone. Visualize divine light descending into the stone and filling it until all negative energies are dispelled. See the light expanding around the stone and emanating from it. Keep your intention firmly in mind to cleanse the stone of any previous negative associations. When you have a true sense that the stone is properly cleared, say a simply word of thanks and release the energy back to its source.

Attuning

Once your new gem is cleansed it is time to begin the process of getting acquainted. It is a good idea to handle the stone a great deal during this process. Remember that you are building a relationship of pure energy between yourself and the stone. This is a partnership of sorts and should be approached with respect and reverence. It is a personal decision whether or not to allow others to handle your magickal tools, but even if you might do so in the future, during the process of bonding with the stone it is ideal to let no one else touch it. You don't need energies other than your own influencing at this stage.

There are many things you can do to encourage your stone to attune to your own personal energies. Sleep with the stone under your pillow for three nights. Carry the stone on your person for three days to a week. Perform a meditative journey within the stone. You can come up with your own ideas, but the point is to keep it with you, interact with it, and generally just allow it to accustom itself to you. It may not be a living thing in the traditional sense, but stones have an energy all their own. It needs to be respected, so patience is necessary here.

From a purely mundane standpoint, it is a good idea to get to know your stone visually as well. You might consider using a jeweler's loupe for this. A loupe is simply a small magnifying glass used by jewelers and watchmakers. You can find them at hobby stores, some jewelry stores, and you can certainly order them online. If you don't have or don't want to buy a loupe, any hand held magnifying glass will work as well. Hold the stone in front of a light source while you examine it. The edge of a lampshade is excellent for viewing the interior of a gem, so try that. Hold the loupe or magnifying glass between your eye and the gem and move the stone toward and away from the device to focus on different parts. Turn the stone slowly and take note of details within the stone as well as on the surface. Chips, fracture lines, planes within the structure of the gem, bubbles, tubes, inclusions, and the like will become apparent through this process. In fact, each stone is as individual as a snowflake and it can be helpful to be familiar with the ones you choose to work with.

Charging

The last thing to do before beginning to use your stone for magickal work is to charge or program it with the necessary intent. Some indirect methods of charging are to expose the stone to moonlight or sunlight, to place the stone within a circle of crystal points pointing inward, or to leave it atop a crystal plate or cluster that has been programmed to charge other stones. I typically recommend combining one of these methods with the following exercise. This exercise utilizes your personal attention and energies, putting some of you into the process.

Hold the gem to be charged in your hands. Breathe, ground, and center. Visualize divine energy descending through the crown of your head. Allow it to fill your body. As the energy builds, focus your thoughts on the intent you wish to program into the stone. This can be as specific as healing or drawing wealth or as general as "I wish to program this stone to assist me in my magickal work." Either way, keep the idea foremost in your mind and visualize the energy flowing down your arms, into your hands, and filling the stone. See the stone glowing with energy and the purpose that you have given it. Once you feel that the stone has absorbed enough of the energy, visualize the flow reversing up your arms and out through your crown back to the source. Clear and release.

Passive Abilities of Gemstones

There are numerous ways to employ stones for magickal means that simply require that the gem be in the vicinity of, or carried by the practitioner. I have dubbed these methods as "passive" solely to differentiate them from work that requires energy and or ritual, and I will address these simpler uses first.

One fun and informative way to use gems in a passive sense is to read others based on their stone(s) of preference. From what you learn about the properties and correspondences of any give stone, it is possible to divine a little about the personality of the person who is strongly drawn to that stone. This extends to folks that may not have any inclination toward magickal or spiritual uses of gems, but can be 'read' based on their choice in jewelry. Even the metal of a setting speaks to the nature of the person wearing it, so study gems and metals to get a better idea of the true nature of those you encounter.

Small gems make excellent gifts and even better offerings. One practice I adopted years ago is to carry a small pouch of quartz with me on any excursion. Whenever I find a treasure or harvest an herb or component from nature, I leave a stone offering in exchange. This process of giving back ensures continued luck in discovering useful items and leaves the area balanced and with a sense of respect.

Gems and ornamental stones as well as crystals can be incorporated into many ritual tools. Jeweled wands and crystal tipped staves are enhanced and influenced by the stones adorning them. A small crystal stored in a pouch or box with a tarot deck, runes, or other divination tool can serve as an amplifier and assist in the use of that tool.

The most prevalent passive gem use is the one that also is most common on a mundane level. The practice of wearing stones as jewelry or carrying them in pouches, pockets or by other means, is a widespread tradition. In fact, the wearing of jewelry has developed an entire language of its own based on the significance of the stones, metals, and shapes of the jewelry as well as the position worn on the body. The primary example of this in western culture is the wedding ring.

For magickal folks, the art of wearing the appropriate gem in the appropriate place on the body can become an intricate and effective recipe for spiritual enhancement. According to the art of physiognomy, the different parts of the body, head, hands, feet, ears, and each individual finger all have an associated meaning. Combine these meanings with the correspondences of each gem species, and you end up with an enormous magickal vocabulary to pick and choose from. The ears, in physiognomy, represent understanding and learning. Combine this with the spiritual implications of amethyst and wearing a pair of lovely amethyst earrings now serves not only a decorative function, but also opens the wearer to knowledge and information from spiritual sources. The neck's relation to self-control and self-image would encourage the wearing of an appropriate necklace to boost confidence or assist in ridding one of a bad habit. Citrine or amber could work to boost confidence, jasper might work for someone wishing to lose weight, and onyx (real onyx) tends to work for those who need to quit smoking. Combining one philosophy, such as physiognomy, with another, such as stone magick, can have powerful results.

The associated meanings for wrists, ankles, waist, arms, and even toes could be combined with stone meanings for an expansive list of magickal uses. The possibilities for significant combinations are endless. You can study physiognomy in detail, if you like, but it doesn't have to be that complicated. For a more general access to the powers of a given stone, try carrying it in your pocket for a day. Make a small neck pouch to carry the stones whose energies you wish access too or add a crystal or stone to your next bath's water. Both of these methods work well enough.

The last of the passive uses I wish to discuss actually borders on active. Because it deals with the placement or arrangement of stones in one's environment, and doesn't necessarily call for energy work on the practitioner's part, I will include it here for the sake of consistency. This method is the specific arrangement of crystals and stones to attain a specific purpose, perhaps incorporating geomancy, feng shui, and ley lines. Incorporating and synthesizing many of the associated concepts, the active arranging of stones in the environment has been practiced since prehistoric times and utilizes the natural energy pathways of the earth itself. When you combine these theories with crystal and gem magick, the results can be spectacular.

The topic and history of geomancy, megalithic sites, and our interaction with ley lines is well beyond the scope and breadth of this work. If you need more information, however, you can always delve more deeply into the subject. For now, we will address some practical uses and applications for an initial foray into the art of geomancy that you can easily experiment with in your own home.

If we look back briefly to the formation of gems and crystals, we remember that the process exposes them to huge amounts of energy. Existing in their natural local within the earth, our gems were once directly inserted into the web of connecting energy currents and vortices that make up the ley lines of the earth. Even removed from direct contact with this energy circuit, the stones we hold in our possession contain the echo of this network and we can easily learn to take advantage of this.

The flow of energy within a space (for example, your living room) can be read and determined through the use of a pendulum or your own intuition. For starters, get out the pendulum. Clear and release as you would before any magickal work, being certain to breathe deeply and relax thoroughly. With the pendulum held gently but firmly in your hand of preference, extend it before you and move slowly about the room. Take your time and remain relaxed. Take breaks if necessary. Throughout this process, make note of any fluctuations in the pendulum, any areas of rapid movement. Note the direction and strength of movement and any gut feelings you may experience.

Once you have an idea of the nature and flow of energy within a space, it becomes possible to employ your magickal stones and crystals to amplify, direct, and improve energy movement. In areas of high frequency or disturbing 'buzzing' energy, place a grounding or highly absorptive stone and note the differences. In areas that seem to stagnate or rest heavily, crystal points can be arranged with the points themselves lined up to direct the energy flow. In areas for magickal working where more intense energy may be appropriate and useful, try gridding the area with crystals along lines of energy flow and at intersecting points. At this point a visualization of intent and blessing becomes highly relevant and the process extends directly into active stone working.

From a simpler standpoint, add a quartz crystal or protective stone to struggling houseplants for a revitalizing effect. Place protective stones and crystals around an outside garden or arrange them in geometrical shapes around plants or trees. For a truly magickal treat, create a crystal garden, or special area outside that is completely surrounded by intentionally placed stones and crystals. The resulting garden becomes charged and is ideal for meditation, magickal working, and as a temple area.

Before we proceed into more active stone use, I'd like to include a word or two about geometry and the shapes of stones as well as the placement of them. The magickal implications of geometric shape come into play in ascertaining stone associations, but are also used heavily when dealing with geomancy and stone arrangement. Geometric shapes have magickal significance based on their numerical sides as well as historical associations. Most magickal people understand the significance of the circle as a magickal construct and protective shape, but in actuality the magickal circle is a sphere and one of the most sacred shapes in magick.

Stones themselves either exist naturally in geometric forms (crystals) or can be cut, faceted, or carved to display the properties in a more geometric form. The stone sphere is a fabulous example of this and a very powerful magickal tool for protection, energy dispersal (with a slow steady emanation) and also for scrying. The crystal point itself naturally directs the flow of energy and many other geometric forms such as the octahedron and decahedron are found in natural crystal formations.

Placing stones in geometric patterns as well as visualizing three dimensional shapes and patterns accesses the meaning of the shape and adds it to the correspondences of the stone. This technique is used heavily in geomancy and gridding.

Actively Using Gemstones

Here we will discuss the more interactive uses of crystals and gems for magick, energy work, and healing. Because most of this work requires a blending of your own energies and actions with the properties and energies of the stone used, the working relationship and knowledge built during the 'attuning' stage with any gem becomes incredibly important.

While the act of holding a crystal or gem during meditation, visualization, or while dreaming is essentially passive, you can actually change things up a bit by sending your consciousness inward to explore within the stone. This is also an excellent way to increase your bond with the stone and to expand your knowledge of its inner intricacies. This is similar to the art of scrying, where one looks into a crystal sphere in anticipation of visual images. Meditations within crystals, however, where the intent is to visualize yourself within the stone and explore the world there will have dramatically different results. Experiment with both and compare your experiences.

Stones of all sorts have been used in magick as spell components for as long as spells have existed. Including an appropriate gem or crystal in a spell bag, packet, or pouch will imbue the spell with the properties of that stone. In the case of quartz, including a small crystal can do wonders to amplify the energy of a spell and increase the results. But if you're burying or otherwise abandoning the spell pouch, you'll also be losing a crystal that quite possibly was not at all cheap.

As an alternate to placing stones within spell bags as a component, and possibly to save the cost of replacing all those stones that would be buried, lost, or given away in the process, gem elixirs are quite easy to prepare and very effective. To create a gem elixir, simply place the appropriate gem or gems (I recommend combinations of gems for more specific results) into a glass container and fill it with water. Place the container in a windowsill or protected place where it will be exposed to direct sunlight. Leave the container there for one full cycle of the moon (one full month). The resulting 'charged' liquid can be used to sprinkle into spell bags, during rituals, added to bathwater, or used in any manner you would normally use the stone itself. Remove the stones and cleanse them thoroughly before further workings.

One word of caution on gem elixirs. Though gems have been ingested for various 'healing' methods throughout history, many of them are highly toxic and contain poisons. Please do not ingest any elixir containing or having contained any gem that is less than 100% positively identified and proven to be non-toxic. Personally, I see no need to ingest gem elixirs as they serve the intended purpose quite well when used strictly for anointing.

On the topic of spellwork, it is quite simple to use a stone or crystal to store a spell for later use. This is exceptionally useful in situations where the timing is perfect but the need may come later. It is also a great tool to use when performing magick for others. Simply store the spell in an appropriate stone and give the stone and instructions for releasing the spell to the recipient. When spell-storing, I usually work the spell with the stone in the center of my altar. Then as the energy is raised and peaks, I send it rushing into the stone and say something along these lines:

> *Sacred stone, earthen bone*
> *Keep my spell, guard it well.*

When the time comes to release the spell I hold the stone in my palms and speak something to this effect:

Sacred crystal, holding power
Release your magick at this hour.

I didn't create these incantations. I don't know who did. I doubt anyone actually knows, but they've become fairly standard in the magickal world for those who practice crystal and gem magick. You can, of course, use whatever incantations you like. Whatever words you use, make certain your intent is clear and the results will be fruitful.

Another stone spell I enjoy working involves arranging stones representing various aspects of any situation into deliberate patterns on a tray that I fill with sand. This is related to the Zen stone gardens, except that I move the stones with intent toward a magickal goal. The sand facilitates drawing sigils, patterns, and images that are related to my spell. Be certain to verbalize what each stone represents as you place them in the tray. Once the stones are placed, you can use a pre-designed pattern to move them about or rely on intuition and improvisation. It's a spell, not rocket science. It's okay to wing it a little bit.

Gems and stones can also be used for divination and have been many times throughout the ages. From scrying to stone pendulums, stone runes to assigning gems to each Tarot card and reading them as such, it seems that the power of the gem is as tied up in divination as it is in most of the magickal arts. You should feel free to incorporate gems into your own divination as often as you like. Get creative and see what happens.

Of all the potential uses for our crystals, however, the most prevalent and the one with the longest history is most definitely healing. The art of gem healing is inextricably related to the chakra system and the energy network within the body. Crystals are used to balance imperfections and negative manifestations in the body's energy system, and specific gems are used in accordance to their chakra alignment. Stones are used extensively in auric healing and Reiki energy healing and are employed for direct physical massage as well.

To use a stone or crystal during aura sensing, healing, or energy work, the practitioner holds the appropriate stone (based on chakra alignment, intent of working, and also shape of stone in question) in their projective hand as they feel the boundary of the subject's aura. Moving slowly, they test the aura all around the body, relying on intuition and physical sensation to alert them to any abnormality or negative or blocked areas. Should any be found the stone is then moved over the area in a manner to clear the blockage, or energy is directed through the stone, or often both are done in conjunction with strong visualizations. You can practice this technique on a perfectly healthy partner if you wish. No harm can come to anything with this type of crystal healing.

It is possible to try a version of this on your own if you don't have partner. Holding a cleared quartz crystal in your own hand it is possible to move it throughout most of your own aura and get a sense for the 'feel' of stone healing. With a partner, you can take turns sensing and stroking each other's aura with the crystal and compare notes. I suggest trying this both as the subject and the 'sensor,' as the experience from both sides if very tactile and worth a firsthand understanding. Be certain to ground and center before and after, and take a break if you get tired. This is especially important if you're working alone since you may not notice how exhausted you are. Crystal healing is effective, but it does come at a cost, and this cost is usually fatigue.

A more involved method of stone healing concerns placing stones directly on or around a subject and directing energy and intent through the entire grouping. Stones can be chosen intuitively or based on their associated properties and are usually arranged in patterns that represent the work to be done. This method can be used on yourself, on others, and even in conjunction with geomancy to affect the energies of a place. This means that you can heal places, such as a polluted river, and not just people. Bear in mind, however, that healing places is much harder than healing people and takes significant practice.

You can also use crystal healing symbolically with tokens of the intent as a form of modified gem spell work. The art of healing in this manner is sympathetic magick as much as it is crystal and gem magick. It is also extensive and very detailed. For further information and extensive patterns and stone alignments there are several very good books on the market. But, once again, experimentation is key. Practice and you will discover what works best for you.

Stone and gem healing is an art form that can take a lifetime to master. There is no end of new methods to be learned, nor new stones to become familiar with. Each new stone possesses unique qualities and helpful attributes to aid you in your journey. I entreat any reader who feels a strong affinity for crystals and gems to dive in with an open heart and let the stones themselves guide you.

Conclusion

When one steps into the shimmering world of gems and crystals, it is easy to become quickly mesmerized by the sparkle and brilliance they naturally possess. And each stone has its own unique history throughout the world. If you truly become enchanted by the allure of emerald, ruby, or the elusive alexandrite, you are in the company of kings. Should you add to that fascination a little spark of magick then you would only be following the natural tendencies of all our ancestors.

And you'd be in good company. The majority of people wear gems in one form or another, even if it's just the standard wedding ring. It is a short step from there to wearing the *right* jewelry, at the *right* moment and with the *right* intent.

The energy and power stored in the gem kingdom can and will enrich your magickal practice if you allow it to do so. A little gemological knowledge, practical advice, and common sense can have an equally profound effect on how you experience gems. There is a balance between the two, and if the practitioner of gem magick can find a place in their library for a good book on gem identification and a well-written buyer's guide, they will be the better off for it.

I leave you then to discover both worlds as you see fit. There is no end to the possibilities if you decide to explore and experiment a little. For the truly adventurous, I might suggest that you engage in the thrill that is stone hunting and hobby mining. But be warned. Once you take a step down that path, you might become quite addicted and content to wander back toward civilization only when in need of a bath and a hot meal. After all, there is magick to be found in the deep places of the world. It's only waiting for us to discover it.

About the Author

Aislin is of Irish, Danish, English, and Romany (Gypsy) descent. Raised on the Canadian prairies, she spent most of her formative years with her maternal grandfather, following him into his garden and through the woods. He introduced her to the magick of nature. It is the magick of her childhood that has the greatest influence on her today.

Aislin is considered a local expert on paganism, the occult, and astrology. She also teaches some local classes on these topics, though The Winnipeg Pagan Teaching Circle. She has been a Wiccan High Priestess since 2000, and has always made an effort to educate seekers when they ask. She founded The Order of the Sacred Star, a group that specializes in educating Pagans of all kinds as well as any other interested parties. Her own children, both boys, are quickly learning the ways of Wicca and seem to embrace nature's magick with vigor. She is also a professional astrologer and Tarot reader, serving her local community in this capacity as frequently as required.

As a writer, Aislin is the author of *Tarot Deciphered: Understanding and Using the Tarot*, which has become a handbook for those new to the Tarot and its uses. She is also the author of the entire *Ash-*

ling Wicca Series, which is the first series of books to publish any-thing about Ashling Wicca and its teachings.

If you're interested in discovering more about Aislin and her work, connect with her through her blog: http://theorderofthesacredstar.blogspot.com/

www.ingramcontent.com/pod-product-compliance
Lightning Source LLC
Chambersburg PA
CBHW071235140726
47996CB00007B/2616